Finding Colours

Blue

Moira Anderson

www.raintreepublishers.co.uk
Visit our website to find out more information about **Raintree** books.

To order:
☎ Phone 44 (0) 1865 888112
🖹 Send a fax to 44 (0) 1865 314091
💻 Visit the Raintree Bookshop at **www.raintreepublishers.co.uk** to browse our catalogue and order online.

First published 2005 by Heinemann Library
a division of Harcourt Education Australia,
18–22 Salmon Street, Port Melbourne Victoria 3207
Australia (a division of Reed International Books Australia
Pty Ltd, ABN 70 001 002 357).
Visit the Heinemann Library website
www.heinemannlibrary.com.au

Published in Great Britain by Heinemann Library,
Halley Court, Jordan Hill, Oxford OX2 8EJ,
part of Harcourt Education
www.heinemann.co.uk/library

ℛ A Reed Elsevier company

Editorial: Moira Anderson, Carmel Heron
Design: Sue Emerson (HL-US), Marta White
Photo research: Jes Senbergs, Wendy Duncan
Production: Tracey Jarrett

Typeset in 26/32 pt Infant Gill Regular
Film separations by Print + Publish, Port Melbourne
Printed and bound in China by
South China Printing Company Ltd.

The paper used to print this book comes from sustainable
resources.

**National Library of Australia
Cataloguing-in-Publication data:**
Anderson, Moira (Moira Helen).
   Blue.

   Includes index.
   For lower primary school students.
   ISBN 1 74070 287 5.

   1. Colors – Juvenile literature. 2. Blue – Juvenile
   literature. I. Title. (Series : Read and learn).
   (Series : Finding colours).

535.6

Acknowledgements
The publisher would like to thank the following for
permission to reproduce photographs: Rob Cruse
Photography: pp. **5** (all items), **6, 8, 9, 10, 11** (party
hat), **13, 14, 15, 23** (bottle, pencil case); Corbis: p. **17**;
Getty Images/PhotoDisc: p. **18**; PhotoDisc: pp. **4, 7, 11**
(balloon), **12, 16, 19, 21, 23** (globe); photolibrary.com:
pp. **20, 22, 23** (beaks, feathers).

Front cover photograph permission of Tudor
Photography, back cover photographs permission
of PhotoDisc (starfish) and Rob Cruse Photography
(teddy bear).

Every attempt has been made to trace and acknowledge
copyright. Where an attempt has been unsuccessful, the
publisher would be pleased to hear from the copyright
owner so any omission or error can be rectified.

Contents

Some words are shown in bold, **like this**.
You can find them in the glossary on page 23.

What is blue?

Blue is a colour.

What different colours can you see in this picture?

The colour blue is all around.

Have you seen these blue things?

What blue things are there at home?

Toys can be blue.

This teddy bear is soft and cuddly.

Bowls can be blue.

This blue bowl is used for porridge.

What is blue out my window?

The sky looks blue out the window.

The sky is mostly blue when it is daytime and there are no clouds.

This blue car is on the road outside.

It moves fast along the road.

What blue things can I have at my party?

This present is blue.

It has blue paper and ribbon.

Some party hats and balloons are blue.

The hats are made of shiny blue cardboard.

What blue things do I use at school?

There is a **globe** of the world at school.

The blue parts of the globe show the ocean.

This blue bottle is good for keeping a drink.

It is made of **plastic** so it won't break.

What else is blue at school?

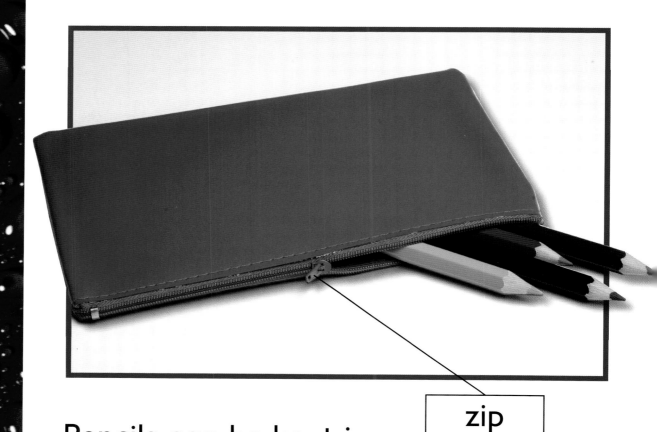

zip

Pencils can be kept in a blue pencil case.

The blue **zip** can open and close the case.

Blue pencils are used at school.

They are good for drawing blue sky.

What is blue at the seaside?

The ocean can look blue
at the seaside.

The water is not very deep here.

These beach umbrellas are blue.

They protect people from the sun.

What blue things do people use?

This vase is blue.

People use vases for flowers.

People use blue ribbons for prizes.

A blue ribbon is for first prize.

Are there blue animals?

beaks

feathers

These birds are blue.

They clean their **feathers** with their **beaks**.

This starfish is blue.

It has a body in the middle and five arms.

Quiz

What blue things can you see at this party?

Look for the answers on page 24.

Glossary

beaks
the hard parts of birds' mouths

feathers
light coverings that grow from
a bird's skin

globe
a ball shape with a map
of the world on it

plastic
a strong, light material that can
be made into different shapes

zip
used to join two bits of material
together; used in bags and clothes

Index

Answers to the quiz on page 22

shirts   dress   hats

bag   cup   balloon

Notes to parents and teachers

Reading non-fiction texts for information is an important part of a child's literacy development. Readers can be encouraged to ask simple questions and then use the text to find the answers. Each chapter in this book begins with a question. Read the questions together. Look at the pictures. Talk about what the answer might be. Then read the text to find out if your predictions were correct. To develop readers' enquiry skills, encourage them to think of other questions they might ask about the topic. Discuss where you could find the answers. Assist children in using the contents page, picture glossary and index to practise research skills and new vocabulary.

Titles in the **Finding Colours** series include:

ISBN   1 74070 287 5

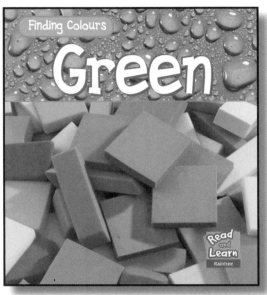

ISBN   1 74070 288 3

ISBN   1 74070 289 1

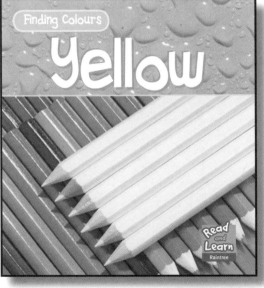

ISBN   1 74070 290 5

Find out about the other titles in this series on our website www.raintreepublishers.co.uk